MAYER SMITH

The Crimson Veil of the Phoenix Queen

First edition

This book was professionally typeset on Reedsy.
Find out more at reedsy.com

Contents

One

The Fireborn Oath

The flames writhed like living serpents, twisting and coiling in the brazier at the heart of the throne room. Shadows flickered against the marble walls, warping the intricate murals of queens past—women immortalized in both fire and eternity. Their painted eyes, dark and knowing, seemed to watch Seraphina as she stepped forward, her crimson veil trailing behind her like a whisper of smoke.

She was the Phoenix Queen, ruler of the Eternal Ashen Court, guardian of the sacred cycle of rebirth. Her people knelt in reverence as she passed, their heads bowed, lips murmuring silent prayers. She was their goddess, their flame, their undying ruler. And yet, beneath the weight of her golden crown, Seraphina felt something stir deep within her—a whisper of unrest, quiet but insistent.

Tonight, she would extinguish a man's life.

It was not the first time she had sentenced a mortal to death. The laws of her kingdom were absolute: any who trespassed upon the holy grounds of the Ashen Palace without invitation would be sacrificed to the flames. And yet, when her guards had dragged the prisoner before her throne, chains rattling against the marble floor, Seraphina had hesitated.

The man before her was not the desperate sort, not the kind of thief or vagabond who foolishly stumbled into forbidden places. He stood tall despite the iron shackles around his wrists, his face streaked with dust but unbowed. His dark, unruly hair fell into his eyes, obscuring a gaze that held no fear.

Seraphina's fingers tightened around the armrests of her throne as she studied him. He was… unexpected.

"State your name," she commanded, her voice steady despite the strange unease curling in her stomach.

The man's lips twitched in something that was not quite a smirk but not far from it. "Caelan Veyne." His voice was low, roughened at the edges, like a blade that had dulled but could still cut deep.

Seraphina narrowed her eyes. "You know the laws of this kingdom, Caelan Veyne. No mortal may trespass upon the sacred grounds of the Phoenix Court and live to speak of it."

"I know," he said simply.

"Then why are you here?"

Caelan's gaze met hers, unwavering. The flames around them hissed, as if impatient for the sacrifice.

"I wanted to see you," he said.

A ripple of murmurs surged through the assembled court. The High Priest, standing rigid beside the throne, inhaled sharply. Seraphina remained still, her expression unreadable, but inside, something twisted. No one had ever spoken to her in such a way.

She let the silence stretch, watching him, waiting for him to falter. He did not.

"Curiosity," she finally said, "is a poor excuse for death."

Caelan tilted his head slightly, considering her. "Then let me offer you another." His voice was measured, careful. "The legends say the Phoenix Queen is eternal, that her body burns and rises anew. But I have studied the old texts, the ones buried beneath dust and time. They speak of something different—of a woman who was once mortal. A woman who—" He hesitated, choosing his words with precision. "—who once loved."

Seraphina's fingers curled against the carved wood of her throne. The court fell silent, the weight of his words pressing upon them all.

It was an old story, a forgotten one.

No one dared speak of the Phoenix Queen's past, not within the palace walls, not within the realm of the living. To question her eternity was to question the very foundation of the Ashen Court.

The High Priest stepped forward, his golden robes glinting in the firelight. "Blasphemy," he spat. "This man seeks to unravel the sacred truths. He must be burned."

The flames in the brazier surged as if in agreement, their heat licking at Seraphina's skin. But she did not look at the fire. Her gaze remained on Caelan, searching. He was not like the others who had come before him—those who had begged, wept, cursed. He stood with a quiet defiance, not of arrogance, but of conviction.

Something in her chest tightened.

She rose from her throne, and the court fell to their knees as one. The heat of the fire pulsed against her skin, but she barely felt it. The golden embroidery of her gown shimmered as she stepped forward, until she stood before him, close enough to see the flicker of flames reflected in his storm-dark eyes.

"Do you seek death, Caelan Veyne?" she asked softly.

His breath hitched for a fraction of a second before he steadied himself. "No."

"Then why risk your life for a story?"

"Because I had to know if you were real," he admitted.

Seraphina's pulse quickened.

The air between them was heavy, charged. She did not move, nor did he. It was foolish, this moment, this hesitation. A queen did not hesitate. And yet…

She lifted her hand. Gasps echoed around the chamber, but she ignored them. Her fingers brushed against his jaw, a light touch, a question. His skin was warm beneath the grime, beneath the roughened exterior of a man who had walked through fire to reach her.

"You should not have come here," she murmured.

"I know," he said again. But this time, his voice held something else. Something unspoken.

Seraphina let her hand drop.

She turned sharply, retreating to the dais where the High Priest watched her with dark, calculating eyes. She knew what he expected. She knew what the court demanded.

But when she spoke, her voice was clear, unwavering.

"He will not burn."

The murmurs turned to shouts of protest. The High Priest's eyes flared with anger. The flames raged higher, greedy and furious.

Seraphina did not waver.

She was the Phoenix Queen. And for the first time in a thousand years, she had chosen differently.

The fire would not take him.

Not yet.

Two

The Forbidden Spark

The air in the Ashen Court was thick with unsaid words.

Seraphina could feel the weight of their stares pressing down on her back like smoldering coals, their whispers a low hum beneath the crackling torches that lined the grand hall. The decision had been made. She had spoken, and the word of the Phoenix Queen was absolute.

Caelan Veyne would not burn.

But that did not mean he was free.

As the guards dragged him through the winding corridors of the palace, his chains clinking against the obsidian floors, Seraphina followed at a measured pace. Her golden robes trailed behind her, her crimson veil swaying like dying embers. She could hear the murmured prayers of the servants as she passed—some in reverence, others in quiet defiance.

She had done something unheard of. She had spared a man who had trespassed upon sacred ground. A man who spoke of things that had long been buried beneath the weight of centuries.

Seraphina's fingers tightened against the folds of her gown. Why had she done it?

It was not weakness. It could not be.

And yet, when she had met Caelan's gaze beneath the flickering light of the throne room, something had stirred within her— something she did not understand, something she did not want to name.

She had seen fear in the eyes of countless men before. She had watched them crumble before her, pleading for mercy they would not receive. But Caelan had not begged. He had not trembled.

He had only looked at her. Like he saw something beneath the fire, beneath the eternity.

The thought unsettled her.

The guards led him into a chamber at the heart of the palace— a circular room carved from black stone, lit only by a single brazier in the center. The light danced against the walls, casting restless shadows. It was a room meant for those who awaited judgment.

A place of neither death nor freedom.

Seraphina entered in silence, her presence commanding the room even as she said nothing. The guards shackled Caelan to an iron post in the center, his arms bound above him, his legs barely able to touch the ground. He winced but did not cry out.

"Leave us," she ordered.

The guards hesitated, exchanging wary glances, but they obeyed. The heavy door groaned shut behind them, sealing them inside.

The fire crackled between them, its light illuminating the sharp angles of Caelan's face—the defiance in his dark eyes, the tension in his jaw. He was watching her. Studying her.

Seraphina hated how aware of it she was.

She stepped closer, her voice calm but edged with something unreadable. "You are either a very brave man, Caelan Veyne, or a very foolish one."

He exhaled a slow breath. "Is there a difference?"

A flicker of amusement ghosted through her before she banished it. "Yes. One leads to glory. The other leads to ashes."

Caelan gave a wry smile, despite the restraints cutting into his wrists. "And which do you think I deserve?"

Seraphina said nothing. She moved to the brazier, trailing her fingers just above the flames. The heat licked at her skin, familiar and alive. Fire did not hurt her. It never had.

"You spoke of old stories," she murmured. "Of things you should not know."

Caelan shifted slightly, the chains rattling. "Because the truth is dangerous?"

"Because it is forgotten," she corrected. "And things that are forgotten are meant to remain that way."

The fire flared as if in agreement, a sudden rush of heat sweeping between them.

Caelan tilted his head, his gaze never leaving her. "Do you fear the truth, Your Majesty?"

Seraphina did not flinch, but something within her coiled tight. No one had ever asked her that before. No one had dared.

"I fear nothing," she said smoothly.

But the words felt hollow.

Caelan's eyes searched hers, as if testing the truth of them. "I don't think that's true," he said finally. "I think you fear what happens if the truth is known. If the Phoenix Queen is not as eternal as they believe."

Her breath caught, but only for a fraction of a second.

Foolish. She should have let him burn.

"Careful, Caelan," she warned, her voice like embers, soft but scorching. "Your tongue is already too bold for a man in chains."

He smirked, though there was something softer beneath it. "And yet, you haven't silenced me."

Seraphina stepped closer, the golden embroidery of her gown whispering against the stone. The firelight traced the delicate curve of her face, the shadow of her lashes, the faint part of her lips as she considered him.

"You think I am cruel," she said.

"I think you are many things," Caelan murmured.

Seraphina reached forward before she could stop herself. Her fingers brushed against his jaw, lingering just long enough to feel the warmth of his skin. It was reckless. Dangerous. But for some reason, she could not pull away.

Neither did he.

"You are a fool," she whispered.

Caelan swallowed, his breath shallow. "Then let me be a fool who has seen you, just once, without the fire in your eyes."

Something in her unraveled.

It was dangerous, the way he looked at her. Like she was not a goddess. Like she was not a queen. Like she was something else entirely.

She should have pulled away. She should have ordered his execution and burned him to nothing but ash.

But she did none of those things.

Instead, she let her fingers linger, let the fire crackle between them, let the silence stretch long enough for something unspoken to take root in the air.

The door behind them suddenly creaked open.

Seraphina did not move, but she already knew who it was.

The High Priest's voice slithered through the chamber, cold and sharp. "Your Majesty," he said, his tone laced with warning. "A decision must be made."

She finally pulled away, turning slowly, masking whatever had just passed between them beneath the mask of a queen.

Caelan said nothing, but she could feel his gaze burning into her even as she walked past him.

She did not look back.

She did not dare.

But the fire had already started.

And Seraphina knew, with a certainty that terrified her, that she would not be able to put it out.

Three

Shadows in the Ashes

The night was restless.

Seraphina sat in her private chamber, staring into the flames of the hearth, her thoughts a labyrinth of unwelcome truths. The scent of burning cedar filled the air, the smoke curling like phantom fingers, reaching, grasping. Outside, the Ashen Palace loomed in the moonlight, its spires clawing toward the heavens, a fortress untouched by time.

She should have killed him.

The thought had taken root, curling around her like a creeping vine, insidious and persistent. Caelan Veyne should have been nothing more than a pile of ashes, carried away by the wind like all those who had trespassed before him.

And yet, he lived.

A man with too many questions, too many dangerous thoughts. A man who, with a single look, had shaken something deep within her, something she had spent centuries burying.

Seraphina exhaled sharply, pressing her fingers against her temples. The palace was quieter than usual tonight. Too quiet. As if the air itself was holding its breath.

A bad omen.

There was a knock at her door.

Seraphina turned sharply, the spell of her thoughts breaking. "Enter," she commanded.

The door creaked open, and one of her royal guards stepped inside, his face grim. His armor glinted under the firelight.

"Your Majesty," he said, bowing low. "The prisoner was attacked."

A cold stillness settled over her.

"Where?" she asked, already rising to her feet.

"The holding chamber. He is alive, but barely. Someone slit his throat."

Seraphina didn't wait for further explanation. She swept past the guard, her robes whispering against the polished floors, the firelight casting elongated shadows as she moved through the corridors. Her heartbeat quickened—not in fear, but in something far more dangerous.

Who would dare?

She reached the chamber within moments, the heavy doors already ajar. The scent of blood thickened the air, mingling with the ever-present heat of the brazier.

Caelan lay on the floor, shackled no longer, his dark tunic slick with blood. His skin was ashen, his breath shallow. The cut at his throat was deep but not fatal—a warning rather than an execution.

Seraphina kneeled beside him, ignoring the murmuring guards at the door. Her fingers brushed against his jaw, tilting his face toward hers. His lashes fluttered, his lips parting as if to speak, but no sound came.

A flicker of something unwanted—something visceral—coiled in her chest.

"You are reckless," she whispered.

His eyes, though heavy with pain, still held that defiant glimmer. "And you are… a terrible queen," he rasped.

She almost laughed. Almost.

Instead, she pressed her hand to his throat, summoning the embers within her. The warmth pooled in her palm, her magic slow and careful as she cauterized the wound. Caelan hissed, his fingers twitching against the stone floor, but he did not cry out.

"Who did this?" she asked.

His breathing was ragged, but he managed a ghost of a smile. "I don't know… Didn't stop to ask."

Seraphina's jaw tightened.

She looked up at the guards. "Double the watch. No one enters or leaves without my word."

They bowed and stepped back, leaving them alone in the dim chamber.

She turned back to Caelan, brushing his blood-matted hair from his forehead. "You are a fool," she murmured.

His smirk softened into something more fragile, something almost… real. "And yet, you keep saving me."

Seraphina exhaled. "Perhaps I tire of death."

It was a lie. She knew it, and so did he.

His fingers, trembling but insistent, curled around her wrist. "Why?"

She could not answer. Not truthfully.

Instead, she rose to her feet. "Rest, Caelan. You will need your strength if you wish to survive the next attempt."

And then, before he could say another word, she turned and left him there, the warmth of his touch still lingering against her skin.

The High Priest's Warning

Seraphina stood before the temple's inner sanctum, where the walls pulsed with the heat of sacred fire. The golden sigils carved into the black stone glowed faintly, ancient and eternal.

The High Priest stood waiting for her, his expression unreadable beneath the shadow of his hood.

"You spared him," he said.

Seraphina met his gaze without flinching. "I did."

"You should not have."

"I decide who burns," she reminded him.

The High Priest exhaled, stepping closer. "This mortal threatens more than your laws, Your Majesty. He threatens you."

Seraphina arched a brow. "You think a single man is a danger to the Phoenix Queen?"

"I think," the High Priest said, "that even gods can bleed."

A silence stretched between them.

Seraphina turned to the sacred flame, watching it flicker, its light casting strange shapes against the walls.

"Someone inside the palace wants him dead," she murmured.

The High Priest did not deny it.

"The Hollow Flame grows bolder," he said after a pause. "There are those who whisper of your rule, who claim that your eternity has lasted long enough."

Seraphina's fingers curled against the stone altar.

"You believe them?" she asked.

"I believe that a kingdom must always fear its ruler," he said. "And if they do not, then it is only a matter of time before fire turns to ash."

His meaning was clear.

Seraphina turned back to him, her voice quiet but sharp. "Find out who gave the order to kill him."

"And if it is one of your own?"

Her expression did not waver. "Then they burn."

The High Priest nodded.

Seraphina turned, walking away from the temple, but the weight of his words followed her.

Even gods can bleed.

A Fire That Cannot Be Extinguished
   She returned to the palace in the dead of night. The corridors were quiet, the torches burning low. She should have retired to her chambers, should have shut the door and let the night pass in silence.

But instead, her feet carried her elsewhere.

To him.

The chamber was dark when she entered, save for the dying embers in the brazier. Caelan was still there, his breathing steadier now, his wounds healing. But he was awake.

Waiting.

She did not speak. Neither did he.

She simply walked forward, the flickering light casting golden reflections against his skin. He watched her, the intensity of his gaze something she felt rather than saw.

Seraphina knelt beside him, close enough to feel the warmth of him, close enough to hear the quiet hitch in his breath.

"You should fear me," she murmured.

Caelan exhaled a soft, humorless laugh. "I should."

She reached out, brushing her fingers against the rough stubble along his jaw.

And yet, she did not stop.

Neither did he.

The fire between them had started long before this moment. And Seraphina knew, with a certainty that both thrilled and terrified her—

It would not go out.

Not now.

Not ever.

Four

Embers

T he evening air was cool, a stark contrast to the firestorm that raged within Seraphina's chest. The grand hall of the Ashen Court was alive with flickering light, the braziers casting shadows that danced like spirits on the marble floors. The guests, robed in silks and velvet, moved like silent phantoms, their laughter hushed by the weight of ancient traditions. Tonight, the Phoenix Queen would hold a feast—an event to mark her reign, to celebrate her eternity.

But Seraphina had never felt more distant from her own throne.

As she walked through the grand hall, her golden gown shimmering in the low light, every step felt heavier than the last. Her crown, a delicate work of gilded fire, sat like a vice on her head. The weight of the jewel-encrusted circlet pressed against her temple, yet it was nothing compared to the storm brewing in

22

her heart.

Caelan had survived his second attempt on his life. His wounds had been healed, and he was no longer chained. But neither was he free.

He had been placed under the strictest guard, but Seraphina knew that was no longer enough. The Hollow Flame was drawing closer, and they would not stop until she was toppled. Or worse.

Tonight's feast, meant to be a moment of celebration, was instead a fragile shield. Her people needed to see their queen as eternal, as infallible. And yet, even as she entered the grand hall, her eyes searched for him. Caelan.

A fool. He had never belonged here.

She had no reason to care about him. He was a mortal, a spark in a world that demanded nothing but ashes. Yet, when his gaze had met hers across the chamber that night—after the blood, after the danger—something had shifted between them. Something she could not control.

Seraphina's eyes scanned the crowd, the music of violins and the murmur of guests fading into the background. Her mind was elsewhere.

And then, she saw him.

He stood near one of the darkened archways, his figure silhouetted against the flickering light, the shadows falling across him like a cloak. Caelan. His dark hair was still a little tousled, his expression unreadable, but his eyes—those eyes—caught hers instantly.

A spark.

He had never looked so… alive.

The moment their gazes met, Seraphina felt it—a pulse in the air, an invisible thread connecting them, a silent recognition that echoed between them. She quickly turned her head, swallowing the sudden surge of heat in her chest. No.

She could not.

She should not.

As her eyes drifted away, the sound of the feast returned to her—laughter, clinking goblets, the shuffle of feet on stone. But Caelan's presence lingered, like smoke that wouldn't clear. It was there in the periphery, tugging at the edge of her focus. Every step she took seemed to draw her back to him, until she finally reached the dais where the throne awaited her.

A hundred eyes turned to watch her ascend, to watch her sit in judgment. The weight of their expectation settled over her, cold and suffocating.

The moment she seated herself, a wave of tension seemed to ripple through the hall. The feast had begun, but no one truly ate. Their eyes were on their queen. They watched her every move, waiting for a sign—an omen. They would not be satisfied until she burned like the legends promised.

And yet, Seraphina felt only a deep weariness in her bones. The fire that had once been her birthright now smoldered like embers, distant and fading.

Her attention wandered again. Her gaze slipped toward Caelan, still standing near the archway, his gaze still locked on her. His presence was like an anchor pulling her deeper into something she did not understand.

For a brief moment, their eyes met again. No words passed between them, but the silence felt louder than any declaration. Caelan didn't need to speak to know the truth that lay between them. She was trapped.

As if in response, the room seemed to grow colder. The distant clang of metal echoed from the courtyard. Seraphina felt her pulse quicken. The Hollow Flame was close.

The High Priest was at her side before she could make sense of her thoughts. His presence was a stark contrast to the warmth of the feast, his sharp eyes watching her with the precision of a blade.

"Your Majesty," he murmured, low enough for only her ears. "There is news."

Seraphina's eyes never wavered from Caelan. "What news?"

"The rebels are closer than we feared. They grow bold in their whispers. Soon they will move." The High Priest's voice was thick with urgency. "We must act before they can strike."

"Not tonight," Seraphina said, her tone sharp, though her mind was elsewhere. She needed to keep the image of the queen intact. Tonight's feast had to be a show of strength. The Hollow Flame could not have its victory, not now.

"Tonight is already a risk," the High Priest pressed. "They are biding their time, but it is clear—they do not fear you, Your Majesty. They have begun to speak of rebellion openly."

Seraphina's fingers tightened on the armrest of her throne. They do not fear me.

Her gaze shifted once more to Caelan. For the briefest of moments, he smiled. A quiet thing, barely a flicker of expression, but enough to make her heart skip. The smile of a man who believed he could win.

The music grew louder, a sharp contrast to the building tension. The violins swelled in a frantic crescendo, their melody winding through the air, pulling Seraphina from her thoughts. She was still on display, still a figure of power, but it felt like a mask now—nothing more than a fragile veil hiding the truth beneath.

Caelan was no fool. He knew what he was doing. By being here, by standing just outside her reach, he had already become part of the game.

But what game was it?

He had survived the assassination attempt. He had fought against his fate, and she—she had let him. Why?

Her breath caught. She couldn't afford to entertain these thoughts. She was the Phoenix Queen, and nothing could threaten her reign.

But when she saw Caelan again, across the chamber, standing in the low light with his eyes burning through her like the last embers of a dying fire, she wondered if that might be the one thing that could burn her down.

The next moment was a blur.

The doors to the grand hall burst open with a loud crack, and the room fell silent. The intruder was swift, dressed in the black robes of the Hollow Flame, his face obscured by the cowl of his hood. He carried a small, ornate dagger, its edge gleaming in the torchlight.

The guards reached for their weapons, but the man was already moving, his steps a blur of purpose. He lunged toward Seraphina's throne.

A gasp rippled through the room.

The world slowed for a heartbeat as Seraphina rose from her seat, her pulse quickening—not with fear, but with something darker. Something primal.

The assassin was almost upon her when Caelan was there, stepping into the path of the blade, his hand gripping the man's wrist in a flash of movement.

The room exploded into chaos.

Caelan's eyes met Seraphina's in that single moment. He was no longer the prisoner, no longer the fool. He was a man who had made a choice. And now, he was fighting for her.

Her heart skipped a beat, and the world went silent.

It was too late. The fire had already started.

Five

The First Betrayal

The night was heavy, thick with the scent of rain that hadn't yet fallen, hanging in the air like a warning. The stone walls of the Ashen Palace stood silent and imposing against the restless dark, their edges blurred by the mist that crawled from the edges of the kingdom. The world outside seemed to hold its breath, waiting.

Seraphina stood on the balcony of her chamber, the breeze tugging at the hem of her gown, the silver moonlight bathing her in a soft, almost ghostly glow. Below, the courtyards sprawled out, empty and silent under the creeping fog.

She should have been focused on the war at hand, on the rebel factions that were steadily growing bolder with each passing day. She should have been thinking of how to tighten the noose around the Hollow Flame, how to keep her kingdom intact. But tonight, her thoughts refused to obey.

They kept returning to him.

Caelan.

Even now, as she stood alone in the stillness, she could feel the imprint of his touch—the weight of his eyes when they had locked in the grand hall, his presence like fire in her veins, burning without mercy.

He had saved her life.

Or had he?

The assassin had come for her, but in the chaos, it had been Caelan who had leapt into the fray. Her guards had acted swiftly, disarming the intruder, but it was Caelan's intervention that had stopped the blade. A simple, unspoken choice. He had made it for her.

The fire had already started. It was a dangerous game, one she had not chosen, but one she now found herself caught in.

Her fingers tightened against the stone railing as she stared out into the distance, her thoughts tangled. She should never have spared him.

And yet, she could not regret it.

The door behind her creaked open.

Without turning, she knew who it was. Her presence was enough for him to find her in the dark, to understand that she was already waiting.

"Your Majesty," came the low voice of the High Priest, his tone clipped, his presence heavy in the room.

She did not respond immediately. Instead, she continued to gaze out over the kingdom. The fog was thickening, clinging to the towers of the palace like a shroud. A storm was coming.

"The Hollow Flame is moving faster than we anticipated," he continued, stepping into the room, his dark robes brushing the floor like whispers. "We have confirmed reports of their plans—an attack is imminent."

Seraphina finally turned to face him, the cool wind tousling her hair. Her gaze flickered over him with little interest. "We will deal with it as we always have," she said softly, but there was an edge to her voice, something dark and unspoken.

The High Priest stepped closer, his eyes narrowed. "And what of the mortal, Caelan? You still choose to protect him?"

Seraphina's heart skipped a beat, the words like a knife cutting through the fog of her thoughts. "He is of no concern to you."

The High Priest's lip curled into something close to a smile, though it lacked any warmth. "It should be. You risk everything by letting him live. The people already whisper. They speak of rebellion, of the Queen who has let a man—a mortal—infiltrate her court, her heart."

The air between them seemed to chill, a sudden, sharp coldness filling the room. Seraphina clenched her fists, the flames inside her flickering dangerously.

"I will not be controlled by whispers," she said, her voice steady, but there was a tremor beneath it. She took a deep breath. "I do what I must. Nothing more, nothing less."

The High Priest's gaze lingered on her for a moment, studying her with the kind of intensity that made her skin prickle. He knew something—he always knew something—but for once, she wasn't sure what it was.

Finally, he spoke again, his tone quieter, more insidious. "You should not underestimate the Hollow Flame, Your Majesty. They are already in your court."

The words hit her like a slap. Her breath caught.

"Explain yourself."

A thin smile played at the corners of the High Priest's lips. "There are many ways to bring down a queen. And sometimes, betrayal comes from within."

Before she could respond, the High Priest bowed deeply, stepping backward with slow, deliberate movements. "I will continue my investigations. But remember, Your Majesty: even fire has its limits."

The door clicked shut behind him, and Seraphina stood alone once more. Her chest felt tight, her heart beating too fast.

She knew it wasn't just the Hollow Flame the High Priest was warning her about. It was her own court.

Her own people.

Seraphina walked to the edge of the balcony again, her mind racing. She had been blind to so many things—her heart, her duty, the growing unrest. Caelan.

But the pieces were falling into place now, as if the world had suddenly shifted into sharper focus. She could not trust anyone.

Not even him.

Λ Heart in the Ashes

The next morning, the tension in the Ashen Court was palpable. Whispers filled the halls like smoke, curling and twisting in every direction. Seraphina could feel the eyes of her people on her, waiting for her to make a move. But she was tired—tired of playing games, tired of the lies, the masks.

She needed answers.

Caelan was still in his chamber, confined but alive, still breathing. But his life had not been the only thing at risk. There was something more in play now, something that no one could see yet. She could feel it, creeping in the shadows.

As she walked through the corridors, her boots clicking sharply against the stone, she couldn't shake the image of Caelan's face in the dim light of the feast hall, his eyes burning with something more than survival. It had been a long time since she had allowed anyone to get close. Too long.

But she had allowed him.

And now, she had to decide what to do with that.

The guards at Caelan's door stepped aside as she approached, the usual respect and fear evident in their eyes. She didn't need to speak for them to know what her presence meant.

The door opened with a quiet creak, and Seraphina stepped inside. The room was dim, lit only by a few flickering candles. Caelan was sitting at the edge of the bed, his back straight, but there was an air of tension about him—something like restraint, like he was preparing for something.

"Your Majesty," he said, his voice hoarse, though it carried no fear.

"Caelan," she replied, her voice a low murmur. "How are you?"

"Alive," he said simply. His eyes met hers, and for the briefest of moments, something passed between them—something too real, too undeniable to ignore.

But she quickly hardened herself, stepping forward, her gaze narrowing. "You risked your life again. For me."

Caelan's smile was small, almost sad. "I risked my life for the truth."

The words cut deeper than she expected. She swallowed hard, the fire within her flickering dangerously. "And what truth is that?"

He stood slowly, his movements cautious but fluid, as though he knew better than to move too quickly. "The truth that I cannot escape, Your Majesty."

Seraphina took a step closer, her breath catching in her throat. His words hit too close to something she wasn't ready to face, something buried beneath the weight of eternity.

"You should fear me," she whispered.

Caelan stepped forward, his voice steady. "I don't fear you. I never have."

She stepped back, shaking her head, the fire in her chest threatening to consume her. She couldn't breathe. She couldn't think.

She couldn't keep him.

Six

The Mortal's Deception

The moon hung low in the sky, its pale light spilling over the Ashen Court like liquid silver, soft and cold. The air had turned thick, almost oppressive, as if the heavens themselves knew what Seraphina had begun to feel—something was shifting beneath her feet, an unseen force threatening to destabilize her world. The mist rolled in once more, veiling the palace in a shroud of uncertainty.

Seraphina stood before the massive windows of her chamber, her silhouette outlined by the dim glow of the moon. Her hands rested on the stone ledge, her fingers tracing the intricate carvings as her thoughts spiraled. It had been days since the attack at the feast, since Caelan had risked his life, again, to protect her. His eyes had been steady in the chaos, his resolve unwavering. And yet, the rebellion was growing. The Hollow Flame was not just a shadow in the dark anymore. It had roots

36

in her own court.

Who could she trust?

Her chest tightened as she thought of the High Priest's words, the veiled threats that lingered like smoke. She could feel his eyes on her constantly, his influence creeping into every corner of the palace. The priests, the guards, her advisors—they were all watching, waiting for her to falter. Waiting for a sign of weakness.

But her weakness wasn't in her power. It was in her heart.

Seraphina's pulse quickened, a strange mixture of fear and longing coiling within her. The fire in her veins burned hotter as she thought of Caelan, of the way he looked at her with those dark eyes, full of secrets and defiance. She should have had him executed, should have let him burn with the rest of the trespassers. Instead, she had kept him close.

Too close.

A knock on the door pulled her from her thoughts.

"Enter," she commanded, her voice betraying none of the turmoil within.

The door creaked open, and a guard stepped inside, his face drawn, his posture stiff. "Your Majesty," he said, bowing low. "The prisoner, Caelan Veyne, has requested to speak with you."

A rush of heat flooded Seraphina's chest, though she did not move. "What is it he wishes to speak of?"

The guard hesitated, his eyes flickering nervously. "He claims it is urgent, Your Majesty. He says it pertains to the Hollow Flame. And…" He faltered, as if uncertain how to proceed. "And the truth."

Seraphina's breath caught. The truth.

She pushed herself away from the window and straightened, regaining her composure. The room felt too small, too constricted for the thoughts that raced through her mind. "Let him in."

The guard nodded and withdrew.

Moments later, Caelan was standing in the doorway, his dark hair tousled, his clothes still bearing the remnants of his last battle. He stood tall, defiant, as always, but there was something in his eyes that unnerved her. It wasn't fear or uncertainty. It was something far more dangerous—awareness.

Seraphina's pulse quickened again, but she didn't let it show. "You have come to beg for your life, then?"

Caelan's lips quirked into a small, knowing smile, though it didn't reach his eyes. He stepped inside, the door closing behind him with a soft click. "I came to offer you a choice."

"A choice?" Her voice was tight, controlled. She couldn't afford to show weakness. Not now. Not with everything hanging in the balance.

He stepped closer, his gaze unwavering. "A choice between continuing down this path of lies or… facing the truth."

Seraphina took a sharp breath. "What truth?"

He didn't answer immediately. Instead, he looked around the room, his eyes lingering on the ornate furnishings, the gold accents, the lavish tapestries—the trappings of power. Finally, his gaze returned to hers, dark and steady. "The Hollow Flame isn't what you think it is. And neither are you."

Her heart skipped. His words were a sharp strike against the fortress of her carefully constructed world. She should have told him to leave. Told him that his words were nothing more than reckless defiance. But something in his voice, something in the way he stood before her—daring, unafraid—stopped her from doing so.

"You think you know me," she said, her voice low, almost dangerous. "You think you know anything about me. But you don't."

Caelan's eyes softened, just for a moment. Then his expression hardened again, as if steeling himself against the truth he was about to speak. "I know that the Hollow Flame is not the enemy you've made it out to be."

Seraphina froze. Her breath caught in her throat. "What are

you saying?"

He took another step forward, his presence suffocating, pulling her in like the heat of an open flame. "They're not rebels. They're freedom fighters. And they want you to burn, Seraphina. Not because you are immortal, not because you are a queen, but because you have enslaved your people with the lie of eternal life."

Her heart raced. This was treason. She had to stop this.

She swallowed, the words tasting like ash on her tongue. "You are not welcome here, Caelan. Leave now, and I might still show you mercy."

He didn't move. Didn't back down. "You think you have power. But all you have is a crown. You think you hold fire in your hands, but it's just smoke. You can't control it. You never could."

The words stung more than they should have, and Seraphina felt something shift inside her—a crack, deep and wide, threatening to swallow her whole. She blinked, trying to focus, trying to keep the walls up.

"You are a fool." Her voice was cold, cutting, the only defense she had left.

Caelan's gaze never wavered. "Perhaps. But at least I'm not afraid of the truth."

The room seemed to contract around them, the air thick with

tension. For the first time since he had stepped into her life, Seraphina wasn't sure of anything. Not her power. Not her kingdom. Not her heart.

She stepped back, needing space, needing distance. "What do you want from me, Caelan?"

He tilted his head, his eyes dark and unyielding. "I want you to see the truth. You can choose to continue hiding behind your crown, your fire, your immortality… or you can face what's coming. Because they are coming for you, Seraphina. Not because you are a queen. But because you are afraid."

The words struck deep. And for a moment, she was paralyzed, caught between the weight of his words and the fear they ignited. Afraid.

But of what?

Seraphina couldn't let herself show weakness. Not now. Not ever. "Leave. Now."

Caelan hesitated, his expression unreadable. Then, with a quiet exhale, he nodded. "But know this—your world is built on lies. And the truth will always burn."

He turned and walked out of the room, leaving Seraphina standing in the center of the chamber, the weight of his words lingering in the air like smoke.

The silence that followed was deafening. She could feel her

heartbeat in her chest, steady and fast, like a drum calling her to war. She wanted to scream, to rage against everything he had said. But instead, she stood frozen, her thoughts swirling like the mist outside the palace.

Was he right?

Could she afford to keep ignoring the truth?

She didn't know.

But the fire within her, the one that had kept her alive for centuries, was flickering dangerously close to going out.

And Seraphina knew—if it went out, everything would burn.

Seven

The Chain of Fate

The night was still, too still. The heavy air pressed against the stone walls of the Ashen Palace, the usual sounds of the court—voices, laughter, music—absent, as though the entire kingdom had fallen silent in anticipation. Seraphina could feel the weight of that silence in her bones, the same way one feels the first drop of rain before the storm breaks. The calm before the chaos.

The palace was alive with whispers, but not of the Hollow Flame this time. Tonight, it was about her. About the decisions she had made—the wrong decisions—and the consequences that were now knocking at the gates.

Seraphina stood before her mirror, her hands trembling ever so slightly as she adjusted the folds of her gown, the fabric of gold shimmering with each movement. Her reflection seemed distorted, as if the woman staring back at her wasn't entirely herself. The weight of the crown on her head was more oppressive tonight, the gilded points digging into her temples as if it was reminding her of her responsibility. Of the price she would pay for letting a mortal get too close.

Her breath caught as her gaze lingered on the reflection of her own eyes—dark, heavy, haunted. She had spent centuries building this kingdom, this reign of fire and eternity. And now, it was slipping through her fingers like ash in the wind.

A knock at the door broke the quiet.

"Enter," Seraphina commanded, her voice steady, though her heart was anything but.

The door creaked open, and her most trusted guard stepped inside. His face was stern, but there was something else in his eyes—a flicker of uncertainty, of fear.

"Your Majesty," he said, bowing low. "There's been an incident. It's Caelan."

Seraphina felt her stomach tighten, a cold knot forming in the pit of her stomach. "What happened?" she demanded, her voice sharper than she intended.

"He's gone," the guard said, his voice low, almost hesitant. "He's vanished from his chambers. There's no trace of him."

Her heart skipped a beat. "Gone?" she whispered. "How?"

"We don't know, Your Majesty. The guards swore they were watching him, but—" The guard faltered. "He's not there. His chains are broken."

Seraphina's breath hitched in her throat. This was not supposed to happen. The Hollow Flame was already within the palace walls, but this—this was different. This was something far more personal. Caelan had slipped through their grasp, and with him, so had her control.

"Find him," she said, her voice low but dangerous. "Now."

The guard nodded and quickly withdrew, leaving her alone once more in the heavy silence.

The Fading Ember

The moon hung high, casting its pale light across the court-yard as Seraphina stalked through the shadows, her heart pounding in her chest. Every step she took echoed through the empty halls, the sounds swallowed by the vastness of the palace. The once-gilded beauty of the Ashen Palace now felt cold and oppressive, as though the walls themselves were closing in on her.

She had spent hours searching the palace, her heart burning with a quiet fury. It wasn't just Caelan's disappearance that gnawed at her. It was the sense of being hunted, the feeling that someone was always just one step ahead of her. She had allowed him to slip through her fingers, and now, she was paying the price.

But what was he doing? Where was he?

Her thoughts swirled in a chaotic spiral, and she couldn't stop the questions from flooding her mind. Was he a threat? Had he been playing her all along? Or had he truly been trying to protect her?

Seraphina's steps faltered as her gaze landed on something on the stone floor—a trail of blood.

Her breath caught in her throat.

The blood was fresh, still dark, glistening in the moonlight. It led down a narrow hallway, one she hadn't thought to check. Her instincts screamed at her to turn back, to leave this place before it consumed her completely. But something inside her, something buried deep beneath the layers of her power, pushed her forward.

She followed the trail, each step a silent plea for answers. The blood led her deeper into the palace, into the forgotten hallways that no one dared enter. This was not a place for royalty, but for those who had been long forgotten, who had outlived their usefulness. The walls here were cracked, the air thick with dust and disuse.

At the end of the hallway, she found him.

Caelan.

He was leaning against the wall, his chest rising and falling in shallow breaths, a dark stain spreading across his tunic where the blood had soaked through. He looked up at her as she approached, his expression unreadable, as if he hadn't expected to see her here.

For a moment, neither of them spoke. The silence between them was thick, laden with questions neither of them wanted to voice.

"You shouldn't be here," Seraphina said finally, her voice low and tight, though it trembled just beneath the surface.

Caelan didn't respond immediately. He just stared at her, his eyes too intense, too knowing. He had seen something in her, something she hadn't allowed herself to see. He knew the truth.

"Neither of us should be here," he said quietly, his voice raw with pain.

Seraphina's heart twisted in her chest. There was no time for this. No time for whatever this was between them. Her kingdom was crumbling, and yet here she was, standing in the dark, with a mortal who had somehow, impossibly, stolen a part of her soul.

"What happened?" she demanded, forcing herself to remain composed.

Caelan's lips curved into a faint, ironic smile. "You didn't think they'd let me go so easily, did you?"

She felt a shiver crawl down her spine. "Who?"

"The Hollow Flame." His gaze flickered downward. "And someone else. Someone you trust."

The words hit her like a blow to the chest. Her breath caught, her pulse quickened. "What are you saying?"

Caelan's eyes softened with a look of sympathy, and she hated him for it. "I'm saying that you've been blind, Seraphina. Blind to the true danger. There's more than just the Hollow Flame at work here. There's someone inside your court who wants you gone."

The words reverberated through her, settling like a cold weight in her stomach. Her mind screamed in denial, but her heart— her heart had already known. The High Priest. The whispers. The way things had felt… wrong.

"You're lying," she spat, her voice trembling with fury. "I trust no one more than I trust my court."

Caelan shook his head, a rueful smile playing at the corner of his lips. "Trust isn't something that comes easily, Your Majesty. Not in a place like this."

He winced, clutching at his side where blood had begun to seep through his fingers.

Seraphina knelt beside him, fury turning into something else— something darker, more dangerous. She had been betrayed.

By the very people who were supposed to serve her. But she couldn't let that thought consume her, not yet. Not while Caelan was still here.

"Who?" she demanded again, her voice low but sharp. "Who is it?"

He didn't answer immediately, but when he finally spoke, his voice was a whisper—hoarse, filled with something like regret. "The High Priest."

Her heart stopped.

The High Priest. Her most trusted advisor. The one who had whispered in her ear, who had watched over her for so many years.

No.

It couldn't be.

Seraphina's breath quickened. "No."

But the truth had already been spoken, and there was no going back.

Eight

The Pyre's Final Test

The Ashen Palace was eerily silent as Seraphina walked through its halls, her footsteps muffled by the thick carpet of dust that had begun to settle on the ancient stones. The shadows seemed to stretch unnaturally, curling around her like whispers, creeping toward her every step. The palace, once a place of strength and unchallenged power, now felt like a tomb. Her kingdom, her very life, was on the verge of collapse, and Seraphina had no idea which way the flame would burn.

Outside, the wind howled through the crumbling towers, carrying with it the scent of rain and something darker— something foreboding, as if the heavens themselves were mourning the coming storm. She could almost feel the weight of the world on her shoulders, a weight she had carried for centuries, but now, it felt heavier than ever before.

Tonight, everything would change.

Seraphina paused at the threshold of the grand hall, her fingers grazing the doorframe. The flickering light from the braziers cast a haunting glow across the marble floors, the flames dancing as if alive, mocking her uncertainty. The court was already gathered—noblemen and women, soldiers, courtiers, all waiting, watching. They knew something was coming. She could feel their eyes on her, their gazes heavy with expectation.

The air was thick with the smell of burning incense, the rich scent laced with bitterness. It was supposed to be a night of celebration. But nothing about tonight felt celebratory.

It was an execution.

Her eyes swept across the room. The High Priest stood near the dais, his face as unreadable as ever. Beside him, a table was draped in black velvet, a single candle flickering in the center. The brazier next to it crackled ominously, casting strange, distorted shadows against the walls. At the center of the dais stood a wooden post, the faint marks of previous ceremonies still visible on its surface. The post was meant for those who had crossed her—those who dared to challenge the Phoenix Queen.

And tonight, it was meant for someone she had allowed far too close. Someone who had dared to defy her, even as she had done the same.

Caelan.

She forced herself to move forward, her legs heavy beneath her, the weight of the crown unbearable. He was chained to the post, his head bowed, his shoulders slumped in defeat. The soft hiss of his breath was the only sound in the room, and Seraphina's heart twisted painfully in her chest.

He had come for her again. For the truth. For justice.

She hated him for it.

She hated that, somehow, through his defiance, through his quiet, unwavering resolve, he had made her question everything she had ever believed in.

"You will not be shown mercy," she whispered to herself, though the words felt hollow. It wasn't a promise. It was a lie.

Seraphina reached the front of the dais, and the room fell into a heavy silence. All eyes were on her, waiting for her to speak, for her to make the final decision. But even as she stood before them, she wasn't sure which way she would choose. The truth, or the kingdom she had spent centuries building.

"Seraphina," Caelan's voice broke the silence, low and strained but undeniably defiant. He lifted his head, his dark eyes locking onto hers. "You have a choice."

The audacity of his words struck her like a slap, and yet they made something stir deep within her—something she couldn't name. He was standing before her, bound, broken, yet unyielding. His eyes held that fire again, the same fire that had drawn her in from the very beginning. And, for a moment, she wondered if it was that fire that would be her undoing.

"What choice do you think I have, Caelan?" Her voice was sharp, but it cracked at the edges. She hated that he could still do this to her, even after everything. "You've condemned yourself."

He smiled then, a quiet, resigned smile. "I haven't condemned myself. You have."

The words hit her like a bolt of lightning, and Seraphina felt the ground shift beneath her feet. For a fleeting moment, she thought she might fall. Her chest constricted, the fire within her flickering and threatening to die. She had always been in control, always commanded the flames. But now, standing before him, she felt as if she were watching it slip from her fingers, the heat waning, the smoke swirling around her.

"I gave you everything," she whispered, her voice shaking. "And you used it to bring chaos into my kingdom."

"Your kingdom," he said softly, his voice almost kind, "was never your own, Seraphina. It was built on lies, on a cycle of rebirth that never truly gave you freedom. And you've held on to it for so long, convinced that if you could just keep the fire burning, you'd never have to face the truth."

Seraphina's breath caught, and for a moment, the world around her seemed to still. The flickering flames of the brazier stilled as if listening, waiting for her to make the final choice. She stood there, caught between two worlds—the world she had created, the world of fire and eternity—and the world that Caelan had shown her, the world of truth, freedom, and the consequences of her own choices.

She took a deep breath, her fingers curling into fists at her sides. The room held its breath with her, the tension hanging in the air like a storm waiting to break. The weight of the crown seemed unbearable, and for the briefest moment, she wondered if she could take it off. If she could walk away from everything she had known.

But she couldn't.

She couldn't.

With a snap of her fingers, the guards stepped forward, unlocking the chains that held Caelan in place. The action was swift, but the moment felt endless, the air thick with the unspoken consequences. She had made her choice.

"You are free," Seraphina said, her voice cold but steady. "But know this, Caelan. I do not forget betrayal."

The room seemed to exhale in unison, the tension breaking, the whispers of the courtiers rising like a wave. Caelan took a step forward, his shoulders tense but resolute. His eyes locked onto hers, and for the first time in what felt like ages, Seraphina saw something like understanding in them. No words were exchanged, but the moment stretched between them, heavy and full of unspoken things.

"I don't want your kingdom, Seraphina," Caelan said softly. "I want you to be free. To let go of the chains that bind you."

His words hit her like a dagger to the heart, and she felt something inside her stir, a faint flicker of hope. For a moment, it was almost enough to make her want to believe him. But she knew better.

"Go," she said, her voice quieter now, almost lost beneath the weight of her own conflicted heart. "Before it's too late."

Caelan gave her one last look—his gaze lingering for just a moment longer than it should have. He didn't speak again. Instead, he turned and walked toward the open door, his silhouette disappearing into the shadows.

Seraphina stood alone in the grand hall, the weight of her decision settling over her like a shroud. The fire that had once burned so brightly inside her now seemed to flicker, weak and uncertain. And as she stood there, watching the flames dance in the brazier, she realized something—something that terrified her more than anything.

The fire was no longer under her control.

Nine

The Pyre's Final Test

The winds howled outside, tearing through the royal gardens, stripping the trees bare and casting a chill over the already ominous skies. Rain had begun to fall in sheets, heavy and relentless, as if the heavens themselves had decided to mourn the breaking of an empire. The Ashen Palace felt as though it were holding its breath, its cold, ancient walls wrapped in silence, waiting.

Inside the throne room, Seraphina stood alone before the massive brazier, its flames curling and twisting like serpents, illuminating the room with an eerie, flickering glow. Her fingers ached with the desire to feel the heat against her skin, to drown out the cold creeping through her bones. The fire had always been her strength—her life, her power—but now, it felt as though the flames mocked her, flickering with a hollow light that only deepened the darkness inside her.

The truth had been laid bare before her. The Hollow Flame, the rebellion, the betrayal, Caelan. Every thread of her kingdom's fabric had unraveled, exposing the rotten core beneath. She had chosen this path, had forged a crown of fire, but the weight of it had become unbearable.

Her heart beat faster, the blood in her veins a strange mix of fire and ice. Was it too late to turn back? Was it too late to escape the trap she had set for herself?

Her eyes drifted to the far corner of the room, where the door had just opened. A figure stepped inside, cloaked in shadows.

Caelan.

Her breath caught in her throat. She hadn't expected him to come back—not after the choice she had made, the finality of her rejection. She had told him to leave, to walk away, but here he was, standing in the threshold, his eyes burning with something fierce—something untamable. He had never truly left, had he?

"Seraphina," he said, his voice low and filled with something like a quiet defiance, but there was a hint of something softer in it now. "You called for me."

Her pulse quickened as his gaze locked onto hers, intense, unyielding. His words, his presence, everything about him was like a flame that could not be extinguished, no matter how much she tried to douse it with cold.

"I didn't call for you," she replied sharply, though even she could hear the lie in her voice. She couldn't push him away any longer, not without facing the truth of what she had done.

"You don't have to pretend," he said softly, a wry smile curving his lips. "You can't run from this. From us."

Seraphina felt a tremor pass through her, but she held her ground, her fingers tightening against the cold stone of the brazier. She had to maintain control. She had to keep the fire alive. She had to be the Phoenix Queen.

"Why are you here?" she demanded, her voice a little too sharp, betraying her growing desperation.

"Because I'm the one you've been running from," he said, stepping closer, his footsteps quiet against the marble floor. "Because I see the truth now. And the truth, Seraphina, is that you've been playing a game you can't win."

A heavy silence settled between them, as if the words he had spoken had cracked the very foundation of her world. The flames flickered again, casting shadows that seemed to crawl toward her, toward the dark corners of her soul she had kept locked away. He was right.

"I am the queen of this kingdom," she said, her voice steadier now, though the weight of her words pressed down on her. "And you have no place here."

But even as the words left her lips, she knew they were empty.

She could feel the tension building between them, a force neither of them could ignore. She wanted to scream at him, to demand he leave, but her heart betrayed her. It had always been him, hadn't it? The man who had stolen her attention, her thoughts, from the very first moment. The one who made her question everything she had ever known.

"And yet," he said, his voice a breath against her skin, "here I am. Standing in front of you, because I can't let you burn yourself down."

She flinched, his words piercing through the walls she had built so carefully. She turned away from him, looking back at the brazier, needing the heat to calm her nerves. But it didn't work. It never did anymore.

"Leave," she whispered, her voice ragged.

"I can't," he said, the resolve in his voice unshakable. "Because, no matter what you say, I know you're not the woman you've convinced everyone you are. You're not a queen made of fire. You're someone who's been trapped in the flames for far too long, and you're afraid to let them die out."

She turned to face him, the firelight catching in his eyes, and for a moment, the world seemed to vanish, leaving only the two of them standing in the ruins of her kingdom. She saw the truth in his eyes—his unwavering belief in her, the way he refused to see her as the immortal, unfeeling queen everyone else did. She saw the way he loved her, even now, despite everything she had done.

Her breath caught in her throat.

"You think you know me," she said, her voice breaking. "You think you understand me, but you don't. You have no idea what it's like to carry the weight of eternity on your shoulders." She took a step forward, her hands trembling. "You don't know what it's like to watch everything you care about burn."

"I know that you're suffocating," Caelan said softly. "I know that you're afraid of what will happen when the fire dies, when you have nothing left to burn."

Seraphina's heart lurched in her chest. She wanted to pull away, to shut him out, but the connection between them was too strong. She could feel the heat of him, the warmth of his presence wrapping around her like a cloak. And for the first time in years, she felt the fire inside her flicker, not with anger, but with something else. Something far more dangerous.

"I'm not afraid of fire," she said, though her voice faltered. "I'm afraid of what happens when the fire goes out."

Caelan's gaze softened, and he reached out, his fingers brushing lightly against her arm. The contact was a shock, a spark of something that threatened to set her entire world alight.

"You don't have to do this alone," he said, his voice a whisper. "Let me help you."

She took a step back, her breath coming in short gasps. She couldn't—she couldn't let him in, not like this. Not after everything. She was the Phoenix Queen. She was supposed to stand alone.

But the walls she had built, the fire she had used to protect herself, were crumbling beneath the weight of his words, of his touch. And she knew, deep down, that she had already made the choice.

Seraphina closed her eyes, a tear slipping down her cheek, and for the first time in centuries, she allowed herself to feel the weight of her heart.

"Do you love me, Seraphina?" Caelan's voice was barely more than a breath against her ear.

Her chest tightened, the answer already known, but unspoken. She wanted to say no. She wanted to push him away, to return to the fire that had always kept her safe. But in that moment, standing before him, she realized that nothing she had built, nothing she had burned, could protect her from the truth.

She didn't answer, but the answer was already there, written in the way she looked at him, the way her heart beat for him, even now.

Ten

Lashed

The rain lashed against the palace windows, its relentless fury matching the storm raging within Seraphina. She stood in the dimly lit chamber, the cool air biting at her skin, her gaze fixed on the flickering flames of the brazier. The room felt too small, suffocating, as if the walls were closing in on her with every passing moment. The weight of the crown on her head had become unbearable, pressing down on her like a thousand years of responsibility she had never truly questioned until now.

The fire in front of her crackled and spat, its embers rising into the air like fleeting stars. The warmth it gave off should have comforted her, but it only reminded her of the destruction it could cause, the lives it had consumed over the centuries. She had been the Phoenix Queen, reborn from the flames, the ruler of all things born from fire. Yet now, it felt like the fire was no longer hers to control.

Her eyes flickered to the door, where the shadow of a figure stood, waiting, watching. Caelan.

He had come to her once more, standing just beyond the threshold, his gaze unyielding, filled with a quiet determination that seemed to reach straight into her soul. His presence, so familiar and yet so foreign, settled over her like a cloud of smoke, choking her thoughts, blurring the lines between what she had known and what she feared to admit.

Seraphina knew what he would say. She could already hear his words, his plea for her to see the truth, for her to let go of the chains that bound her. But the chains were all she had left. If she let go of them, what would she be?

"You should leave," she whispered, though her voice trembled despite her attempt at control. The words fell from her lips like a plea, a cry for something—anything—that could save her from this decision.

Caelan didn't move at first. His eyes lingered on her, and Seraphina felt something stir inside her—something that made her heart ache in a way she hadn't allowed herself to feel in centuries. She had built walls around herself, around her heart, to protect the queen that the world needed her to be. But now, standing before him, those walls felt like fragile glass, ready to shatter with a single touch.

"Leave?" His voice was low, calm, but there was an underlying note of something deeper—something like understanding. "You're not running from me, Seraphina. You're running from yourself."

The words hit her like a slap, and for a moment, the world seemed to tilt. She clenched her fists, feeling the familiar burn of the flames rise within her. How dare he? How dare he think he knew what was best for her?

But even as the anger flared, she felt the fear creeping in. The fear of losing herself.

Caelan stepped into the room, his presence filling the space between them, his eyes never leaving hers. The soft patter of the rain against the windows was the only sound in the room now, a quiet rhythm that seemed to match the erratic beat of her heart.

"You have been running for so long, Seraphina," he said, his voice softer now, as if he understood the weight of the words. "But you can't keep running forever. Not from the truth. Not from what you truly want."

The space between them seemed to shrink with every word, every breath. She could feel him, his warmth, his presence pulling her in, and for a moment, she wasn't the Phoenix Queen. She wasn't the ruler of fire. She was just a woman, standing on the edge of something she couldn't name, something she was afraid to fall into.

"I can't," Seraphina whispered, the words breaking from her lips like a confession. She could barely breathe now, the tension in the room thick enough to suffocate her. "I can't let go of the fire."

Caelan's eyes softened, his expression unreadable. He took another step forward, and this time, she didn't pull away. His hand reached out, brushing gently against her cheek. The touch was warm, grounding, and for a brief moment, the fire inside her seemed to calm, the raging storm inside her quieting just enough to allow her to hear her own heartbeat.

"You don't have to," he said softly. "You don't have to let go of the fire, Seraphina. You just need to stop letting it burn you."

Her breath caught in her throat. She hadn't realized how much she needed to hear those words, how much she needed someone to say them—to make her believe it was possible to keep the fire and still be free.

But she couldn't let herself believe it. Not yet.

"I am the Phoenix Queen," she said, her voice cracking, the words coming out as a lifeline. "I can't—"

"Not anymore." Caelan's voice was firm, but there was an undeniable tenderness in his gaze. "You don't have to be the Phoenix Queen anymore, Seraphina. You don't have to be a prisoner of your own power. You have a choice now."

The air between them thickened, the tension palpable. For a moment, Seraphina was silent, lost in the weight of his words.

She had always been the queen, the immortal ruler, the woman made of fire. But now… now, she wasn't so sure.

The fire in the brazier crackled louder, as if in warning, but it no longer held the same power over her. The flames flickered, alive with a dangerous beauty, but they seemed distant, as though they had become something outside of her reach.

"Why are you doing this?" Seraphina's voice was barely a whisper, her eyes searching his for an answer. "Why do you care? You've seen the truth. You know who I am. You know what I've done."

Caelan stepped closer, closing the space between them, and his hand reached for hers. He held it gently, as though he knew how fragile she was, how fragile everything had become.

"I care because I see you, Seraphina," he said, his voice low and steady. "I see who you are beneath the fire, beneath the crown. And that's who I want. Not the queen. Not the ruler. Just you."

Her heart hammered in her chest as his words echoed in her mind. Could she let herself believe it? Could she allow herself to be seen, truly seen, without the mask of the Phoenix Queen?

"I'm afraid," she admitted, the words raw and unfiltered. "I'm afraid of what will happen if I let go of everything I've known."

"I know," Caelan said softly. "But you're not alone anymore. You don't have to face this alone."

For the first time in what felt like forever, Seraphina felt something stir deep inside her. A flicker of hope. A promise. She wasn't sure what it meant, but it felt like freedom.

She took a shaky breath and looked into his eyes—really looked at him—for the first time. There was no judgment in his gaze, no expectations, just a quiet understanding. And for the first time, she allowed herself to believe that it was possible—possible to choose a path that didn't end in flames.

Her hand tightened around his, and the fire in the brazier flared once more, its heat intensifying, but now it felt different—less like a threat, and more like a promise.

Seraphina closed her eyes, her breath steadying as she made her choice.

The Phoenix's Last Flight

The night had fallen like a shroud over the Ashen Palace, dark and thick, the heavy clouds pressing down on the world below. The wind moaned through the halls, a mournful sound, as if the very walls of the palace were lamenting what was to come. The rain, once a gentle drizzle, had turned into a torrential downpour, the heavens weeping for the kingdom that had once been, for the queen who had ruled with both fire and fear.

Seraphina stood at the edge of the palace's tallest tower, her fingers trailing along the cold, stone railing. The wind whipped through her hair, but she barely felt it. The storm in her chest was far greater than any tempest raging outside. Her breath came in shallow gasps as she stared into the night, the dark sky swallowing the stars, leaving only a void. The fire that had burned inside her for centuries, that had been the heart of her immortality, seemed to flicker and die, swallowed by the darkness.

The truth was before her now, undeniable, no longer something she could hide from. Caelan had been right all along. She had built her kingdom on lies, on a cycle that had kept her tethered to the flames, forever bound to a power that consumed everything it touched. But the fire was no longer hers to command, and she had no idea how to stop it from consuming everything around her.

Her heart ached as her thoughts drifted to him—the one man who had walked through the fire to reach her, who had defied the very flames she had wielded as her weapon. Caelan.

She had let him go.

And now, she had to face the consequences.

The sound of the door opening behind her broke through the silence, and she turned to see Caelan standing there, soaked through by the rain, his clothes clinging to his form like a second skin. His eyes, dark and unreadable, locked onto hers, and for a moment, the storm between them seemed to pause, as though the world had held its breath.

"You shouldn't be here," Seraphina said, her voice hoarse, as though she had just woken from a dream she couldn't remember.

Caelan didn't answer immediately. Instead, he stepped closer, his movements deliberate, as though he were testing the distance between them, testing the tension that crackled in the air. He stopped just a few feet away, his gaze steady but filled with something she couldn't name.

"I came because you're lost," he said softly. "You've been lost for a long time, Seraphina."

Her heart skipped, the words like a sting against her chest. "I'm not lost," she replied, though the words felt hollow. "I know exactly where I am."

"Do you?" His voice was low, but there was an edge to it, something that made her stomach tighten. "You think you've controlled everything, but you haven't. You've been running from the truth for too long. And now, it's time to face it."

She felt his words like a blow, even though he hadn't raised his voice. She turned away, unable to meet his gaze any longer. The storm outside seemed to echo her turmoil, the wind howling in protest as it tore through the tower.

"What do you want from me, Caelan?" Seraphina's voice was barely more than a whisper, the weight of her own guilt pressing down on her.

Caelan took another step forward, his presence engulfing her, and she could feel the heat of him, the pull between them that had always been there, even when she had tried to deny it.

"I want you to choose," he said, his voice firm now. "Choose to be free. Choose to stop burning everything you love. You don't have to be the Phoenix Queen anymore, Seraphina. You don't have to be the ruler of ashes and fire."

The words stung, but they were not just an accusation—they were a plea. And in that moment, Seraphina realized something she had been too afraid to face. The power she had clung to for so long had only chained her to a never-ending cycle of destruction. She was the fire, but she was also the ashes. She had destroyed everything she touched, and now, she was standing at the edge of the only thing that had ever mattered.

But could she truly let go?

Her hands clenched at her sides, her nails digging into her palms. She wanted to scream, to lash out at him for daring to offer her freedom when it felt like everything she had ever known was crumbling. But she couldn't. The truth had already taken root inside her, and there was no escaping it now.

"What if I don't want to let go?" she asked, the words raw, the fear she had buried for so long finally breaking through. "What if the fire is all I have left?"

Caelan was silent for a long moment, his gaze softening as he took another step closer, his hand reaching out to gently touch her arm. The warmth of his touch spread through her like wildfire, melting the ice that had encased her heart for so long.

"You have more than that, Seraphina," he said quietly. "You have a choice. You can let the fire consume you, or you can let it go.

But you don't have to do it alone."

Her chest tightened, her breath catching in her throat. She wanted to say something—anything—but the words wouldn't come. Instead, she closed her eyes, the weight of everything crashing down on her. The rain continued to pour around them, soaking them both, but in that moment, Seraphina didn't care. The world outside felt distant, a world she no longer recognized.

She was so tired. So tired of fighting, so tired of the flames that had consumed her for centuries. The Phoenix Queen had been forged from fire, reborn from the ashes, but what would she be without the fire? What would she be without the crown?

She didn't know.

But she knew, now, that she couldn't keep pretending. She couldn't keep playing the role of the queen who burned everything she touched.

Her hand reached up, trembling, and she slowly removed the crown from her head, the heavy weight of it falling from her grasp. The fire inside her flickered, but it didn't die. It simply changed, became something else—something softer, something that didn't burn so brightly.

Caelan reached for her, his hand gentle on her shoulder, and Seraphina felt the weight of his touch like a lifeline. His presence was no longer the force that had once held her in place. Now, it was the thing that had set her free.

"You don't have to be the Phoenix Queen anymore," he whispered. "You can be whoever you choose to be."

She looked up at him, her eyes filled with something she had never allowed herself to feel—vulnerability. The storm outside raged on, but the storm inside her had calmed, just enough for her to see clearly for the first time.

Seraphina didn't speak. She didn't need to. The choice had already been made.

And for the first time in centuries, she felt the weight of the fire inside her lift, like a phoenix rising from the ashes, ready to fly, ready to be free.

Twelve

The Crimson Dawn

The first light of dawn crept over the horizon, spilling into the Ashen Palace like a slow, golden tide. The rain had stopped, leaving the world fresh and washed clean, the air crisp with the scent of wet earth and faint smoke. The sky was streaked with shades of rose and gold, but the color of the world had shifted. No longer was it drenched in shadows; now, everything seemed to pulse with a strange new light, a light that had once been foreign to her.

Seraphina stood at the balcony's edge, the cool morning air brushing against her skin. The wind, lighter now than it had been the night before, tugged at her hair, but it no longer felt like a threat. The palace, still sprawling and imposing, seemed almost diminished in the quiet of the dawn. It was no longer the center of her world, nor was the fire that had once consumed her. That fire had gone out, not in destruction, but in transformation, leaving something new in its wake.

Caelan was standing just behind her, his presence a quiet, constant weight that seemed to balance the air between them. His gaze was fixed on the horizon, but Seraphina knew he was watching her. She could feel the pull of his attention, the way it anchored her, even now, after everything.

It had been hours since the choice had been made. The moment that had unraveled the future she had once believed in. The moment she had taken off her crown.

The Pyre's Final Test had ended not with fire, but with surrender. A surrender that she hadn't been sure she could make, but now, standing on the precipice of a new beginning, she wondered if she had ever truly had a choice.

She had chosen love. She had chosen freedom.

She had chosen to let go of the crown.

"Seraphina," Caelan's voice was a whisper, carrying a softness that spoke volumes of the distance they had traveled together. He stepped closer, just enough for her to feel the heat of him, the warmth that had been there from the beginning, always present, even when she had pushed him away. "Are you ready?"

Her breath caught in her throat as she turned to face him, her heart pounding, as it always did when she saw him. The man who had never asked for anything, who had never once tried to claim her. And yet, in the quiet moments between them, he had become everything she never knew she needed.

"I am," she said, her voice steady, but the words trembled on the edge of something more. It was strange, the way this moment felt so final, as though the world had been held in suspended animation until now, and with this single act, everything would begin again.

He reached for her hand, his fingers brushing over hers. The touch was electric, and Seraphina's heart surged in her chest as she allowed him to pull her toward him, their fingers intertwining. She felt the weight of the decision settle within her bones.

There was no turning back. There never had been.

"Do you ever wonder what it would have been like if we hadn't met?" Caelan's voice was soft, but the question carried more than it should have, more than he intended.

Seraphina closed her eyes for a moment, feeling the wind against her skin, and for the first time in so long, the weight of the world didn't feel so heavy. The chains that had bound her for centuries were gone, and in their place, something new had blossomed—something softer, but no less fierce.

"Sometimes," she replied, opening her eyes and meeting his

gaze. "But then I wonder if it would have mattered. If I had never met you, would I have ever known what it was like to truly be free?"

Caelan's smile was small, almost wistful, as if he understood more than she could say. "It's never too late to find out."

The tension that had held Seraphina's body rigid for so long eased, replaced by something warm and uncertain, yet so familiar. It wasn't the fire that had once defined her, but the slow, steady burn of something that felt like home. Something that pulsed through her veins, igniting every nerve. Something she had always feared—**hope**.

And with it came the knowledge that she was no longer alone. She had a choice, a chance to build something that wasn't tethered to the fire, something that would survive even when the flames were gone.

"I'm ready for this," Seraphina whispered, her words quiet but certain. "I'm ready for what comes next."

The sky outside had turned from soft pink to a deeper crimson, the first rays of sunlight streaking through the clouds, casting the world in a strange, new light. It was as though the heavens themselves were waiting, watching, for something to change.

As if on cue, a low rumble echoed through the palace—distant, but unmistakable. The earth itself seemed to respond, as though it were acknowledging the shift in the balance of power.

The Hollow Flame had risen. The rebellion that had festered beneath the surface of her reign was ready to take form. But Seraphina knew, in that moment, that she was no longer afraid. The world would burn, yes, but it would also be reborn, not from the ashes, but from the choice to rise again. To choose something different.

To choose love.

"Do you think they'll come for us?" she asked, her voice steady, though the question hung heavy in the air.

"They will," Caelan replied, his voice low, a note of resolve settling in. "But we won't be alone."

Seraphina turned away from him, stepping to the edge of the balcony, feeling the weight of her decision settle in her bones. The storm was not over; in fact, it had just begun. But the fear that had once crippled her, the fear of losing everything, was gone. She no longer cared about the things that once held her in place—the crown, the throne, the kingdom.

All she cared about now was what lay ahead, and the man who stood behind her, who had never stopped believing in her.

The fire was gone, but the world was still waiting for her.

Seraphina took a deep breath and stepped forward, the wind lifting her hair, the weight of the past falling away like ashes.

She didn't need to look back to know that Caelan was with her. She could feel him, his steady presence at her side, his hand close enough to reach for when she needed it.

Together, they would face whatever came next. Together, they would rebuild.

The phoenix had risen, not from the flames, but from the choice to live.

And for the first time, Seraphina felt free.